~ Celebrity Influencers ~

MATT DAMON

MARY HERTZ SCARBROUGH

Rourke Educational Media
A Division of Carson Dellosa Education
rourkeeducationalmedia.com

ROURKE'S **SCHOOL to HOME** CONNECTIONS

BEFORE AND DURING READING ACTIVITIES

Before Reading: *Building Background Knowledge and Vocabulary*

Building background knowledge can help children process new information and build upon what they already know. Before reading a book, it is important to tap into what children already know about the topic. This will help them develop their vocabulary and increase their reading comprehension.

Think about it...

1. Why do people enjoy paying attention to celebrities?
2. What is this celebrity famous for?
3. What are some of the qualities about celebrities that make them stand out?
4. What are the similarities and differences between a celebrity and a hero/heroine?
5. How does a person's professional career connect them to personal experiences?
6. How does what we know about the world shape the way we view ourselves?
7. How do our personal experiences shape our view of others?
8. How does the media shape our view of the world and ourselves?

Vocabulary: *Vocabulary Is Key to Reading Comprehension*

Use the following directions to prompt a conversation about each word.

- Read the vocabulary words.
- What comes to mind when you see each word?
- What do you think each word means?

Vocabulary Words:

- *hygiene*
- *microloans*
- *passion*
- *poverty*
- *refugees*
- *tap*

During Reading: *Reading for Meaning and Understanding*

To achieve deep comprehension of a book, children are encouraged to use close reading strategies. During reading, it is important to have children stop and make connections. These connections result in deeper analysis and understanding of a book.

Close Reading a Text

During reading, have children stop and talk about the following:

- Any confusing parts
- Any unknown words
- Text to text, text to self, text to world connections
- The main idea in each chapter or heading

Encourage children to use context clues to determine the meaning of any unknown words. These strategies will help children learn to analyze the text more thoroughly as they read.

When you are finished reading this book, turn to the next-to-last page for **After Reading Questions** and an **Activity**.

Table of Contents

We All Need Water

Actor, producer, and screenwriter Matt Damon learned about the need for clean, safe water around the world. He began to raise money. The money helped bring water to people who needed it.

hygiene (HYE-jeen): the practice of keeping yourself and things around you clean in order to stay healthy

Water Worries

There are three kinds of water issues: unsafe or inadequate drinking water, poor sanitation (toilet issues), and a lack of water for **hygiene.**

Massive Problem

More than two billion people lack safe water at home. There are more than seven billion people in the world.

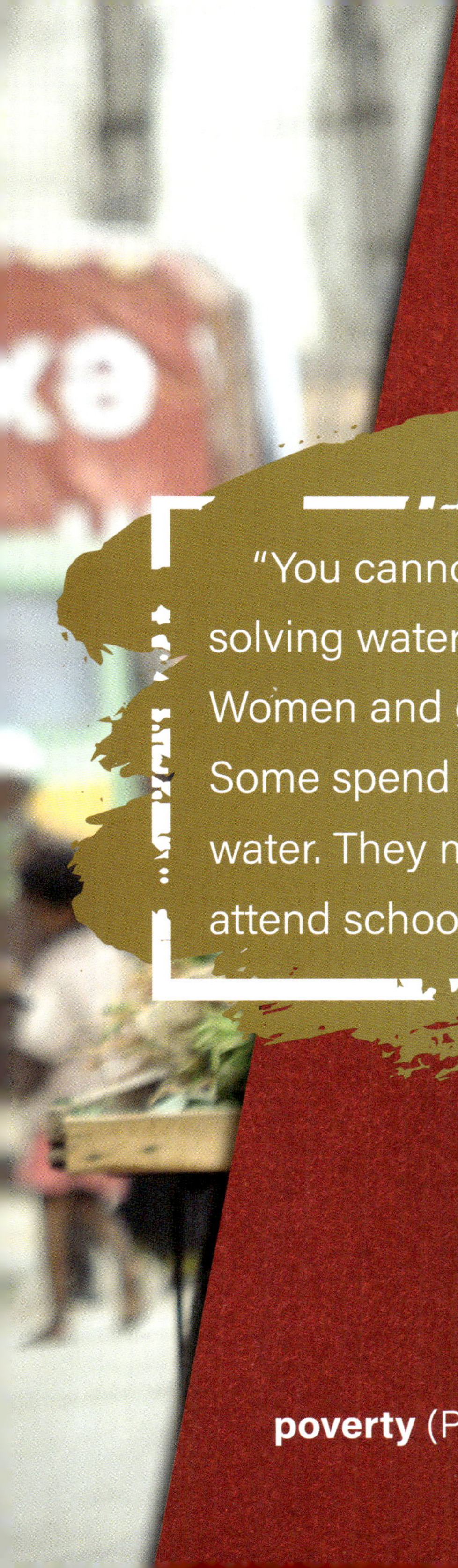

"You cannot solve **poverty** without solving water and sanitation," Matt said. Women and girls are most affected. Some spend six hours a day collecting water. They may not be able to work or attend school.

poverty (PAH-vur-tee): the state of being poor

Matt started an organization called H_20 Africa. It raised money and awareness of water issues. After a while, he wanted to do more. He explored new ideas. He partnered with an experienced water expert.

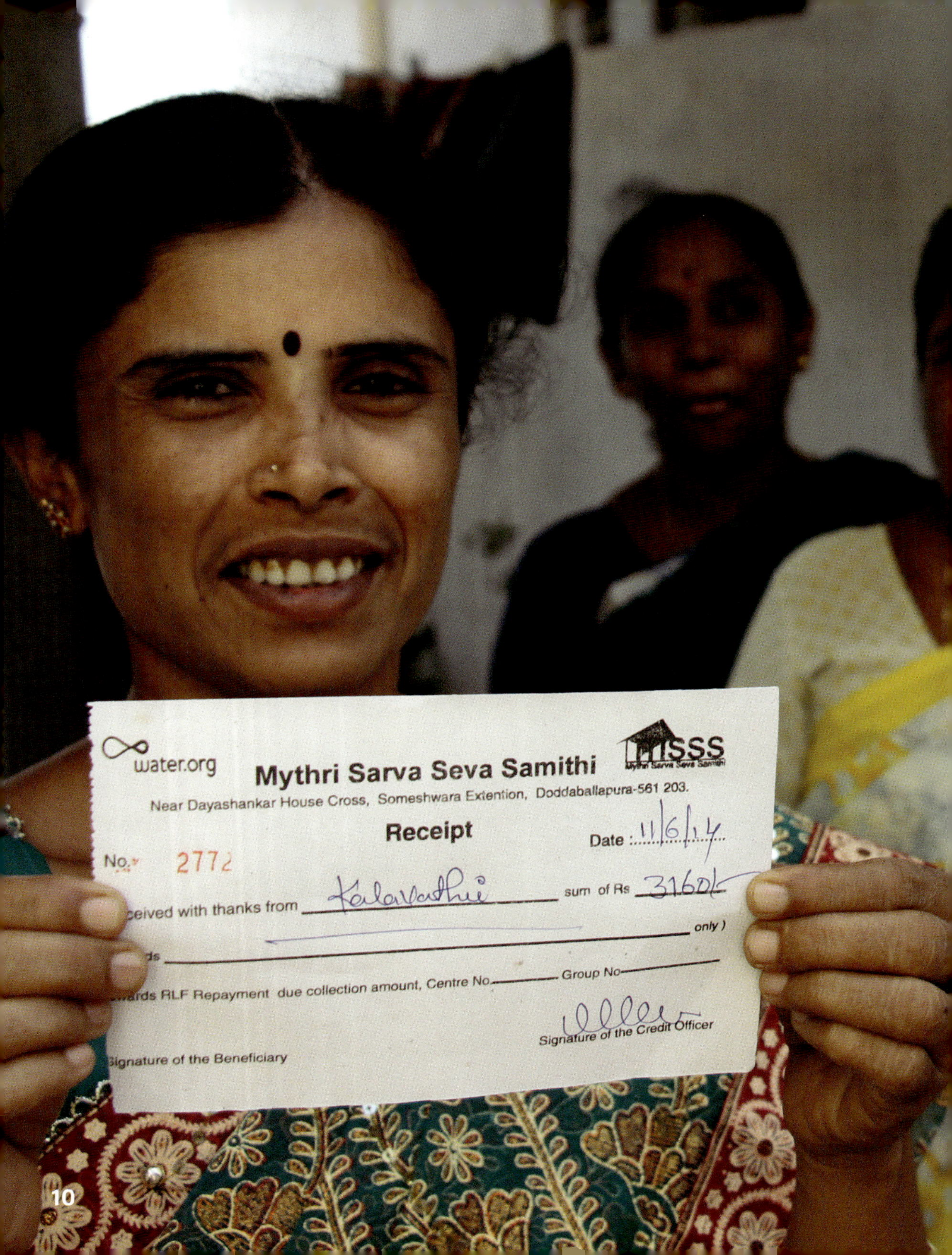
water.org
Mythri Sarva Seva Samithi
MSSS
Near Dayashankar House Cross, Someshwara Extention, Doddaballapura-561 203.
Receipt
Date : 11/6/14
No. 2772
ceived with thanks from Kalavathi
sum of Rs 3160/-
only)
wards RLF Repayment due collection amount, Centre No
Group No
Signature of the Credit Officer
Signature of the Beneficiary

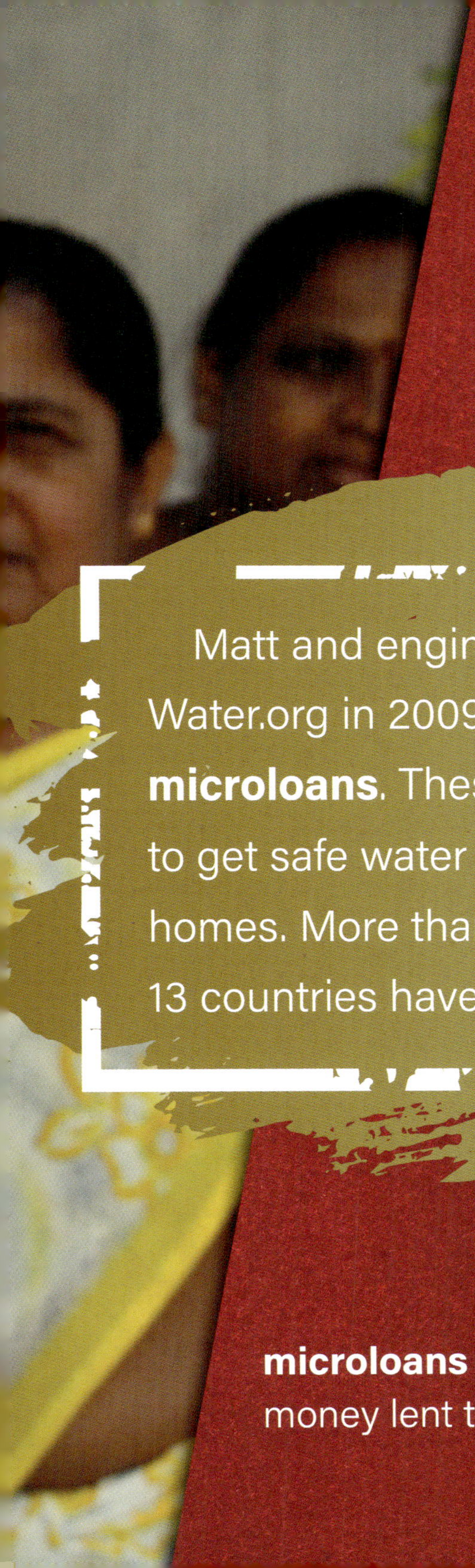

Very Common Problem

Sanitation issues affect 4.5 billion people. Many of those don't have a toilet at home.

Matt and engineer Gary White started Water.org in 2009. This nonprofit makes **microloans**. These loans enable people to get safe water and sanitation in their homes. More than 17 million people in 13 countries have been helped.

microloans (MYE-kroh-lohnz): small amounts of money lent to people or businesses

Matt loves meeting people who have been helped by Water.org. A 13-year-old girl told him she now has time to play. But millions of children still spend their days fetching water. This motivates Matt to keep working.

Hygiene Challenges

Handwashing requires access to water and soap. In some places, less than 25 percent of people have this luxury.

Water.org uses many methods to help people. A mother in India used her loan to install a water **tap**. A woman in Kenya installed a system to catch rainwater. Their lives have improved.

tap (tap): a faucet

Matt realized long ago that solving global water issues is complicated. This challenge will last his entire life. He works with other organizations and causes too. But Water.org is his main **passion**.

passion (PASH-uhn): an object of great enthusiasm or interest

Water Problems Cause Deaths

Diarrhea kills nearly 850,000 every year. This includes many children. Unsafe drinking water, a lack of sanitation, and poor hygiene are three big causes.

Diversity and Gender Equality

The work Matt does with Water.org greatly affects women. Almost 90 percent of the people who borrow money from its programs are women. Almost every woman repays her loan.

ಗ್ರಾಮೀಣ್ ಫೈನಾನ್ಷಿಯಲ್ ಸರ್ವೀಸಸ್ ಪ್ರೈ. ಲಿ.
ಗ್ರಾಮೀಣ್ ಕೂಟ

Matt has been criticized about his movies' lack of diversity. He has started adding diversity riders to his contracts. This requires movie studios to hire many different people, including women and people of color.

What's a Diversity Rider?

A diversity rider promises that the cast and crew will look more like the world around them.

Matt appeared with the cast of the 2017 film Suburbicon.

Humanitarian Issues

Matt works on behalf of Feeding America. This organization has 200 food banks, 60,000 food pantries, and meal programs. Matt played a person needing help in a commercial to advertise food pantries.

Many Are Helped

About one in seven Americans gets some help from Feeding America programs. This adds up to 4.3 billion meals a year.

Matt has also worked on behalf of ONEXONE. This organization tries to improve the lives of children in the United States, Canada, and other countries. It focuses on water, health, education, play, and nutrition.

Matt is one of the founders of Not On Our Watch (NOOW). It supports human rights around the world. He traveled to Zimbabwe in 2009. He went to bring attention to a dire situation there for **refugees**.

refugees (ref-yuh-JEEZ): people who must leave their homes due to war, a natural disaster, or persecution

Good Company

George Clooney, Don Cheadle, and Brad Pitt are also celebrity founders of NOOW. NOOW was renamed The Sentry in 2019.

It's not all hard work and no play for Matt. He has participated in charity poker tournaments with other celebrities. Proceeds went toward projects in Africa.

Memory Game

Look at the pictures. What do you remember reading on the pages where each image appeared?

Index

After Reading Questions

1. What do you think is Matt Damon's biggest accomplishment?
2. How does a person's professional career connect them to personal experiences?
3. Did you learn anything about Matt Damon that surprised you?
4. How do celebrities influence and inspire change?
5. How did the book change your belief about something?

Activity

If you were going to work for Water.org, what kind of job would you like to do? Would you want to work with people who are applying for and receiving microloans? Perhaps you would like to raise money, or be the accountant in charge of making sure money is spent carefully. Or maybe you would like to educate people about water problems. Explain to a friend what your ideal job would be.

About the Author

Mary Hertz Scarbrough's number one reason for writing nonfiction is that she loves to learn new things. She learned a lot about water, poverty, and health as she researched this book. She also loves being inspired by people who are trying to make the world a better place. When her two rescue dogs aren't distracting her, she researches and writes from her home in South Dakota.

www.rourkeeducationalmedia.com

PHOTO CREDITS: Cover: ©Ian West / AP Images; pages 4-5, 30: ©J. Adam Huggins / water.org; pages 6-7: ©Heather Arney / water.org; pages 8-9, 30: ©journalturk; pages 10-11: ©Nick Lundgren / water.org; pages 12-13, 30: ©Annie DeGraff / water.org; pages 14-15: water.org; pages 16-17: ©Gary White / water.org; pages 18-19, 30: Michael Rosen / water.org; pages 20-21: ©Featureflash Photo Agency / shutterstock; pafes 22-23: ©fstop123; pages 24-25, 30: ©FatCamera; pages 26-27: ©hikrn / shutterstock; pages 28-29: ©mediaphotos *Every effort has been made to contact copyright holders of material reproduced in this book. Any omissions will be reflected in subsequent printings if notice is given to publisher.*

Edited by: Kim Thompson
Cover and interior design by: Rhea Magaro-Wallace

Library of Congress PCN Data

Matt Damon / Mary Hertz Scarbrough
(Celebrity Influencers)
ISBN 978-1-73161-732-3 (hard cover)
ISBN 978-1-73161-268-7 (soft cover)
ISBN 978-1-73161-744-6 (e-Book)
ISBN 978-1-73161-756-9 (ePub)
Library of Congress Control Number: 2019932370

Rourke Educational Media
Printed in the United States of America,
North Mankato, Minnesota